The New Arrival

In the United States

Stories and Activities for Language Development

Second Edition

ALEMANY PRESS
REGENTS/PRENTICE HALL
Englewood Cliffs, New Jersey 07632

Project Editor:	Helen Munch
Copy Editor:	Deborah Kransberg
Production / Design:	E. Carol Gee

| Cover Art: | Cesar Natividad |
| Interior Art: | Zahid Sardar |

Acknowledgments   Special thanks to the following: Steven DeBonis, who shared the better half; Kathleen Corey, a friend and a rarity in today's world; the Kuntz, DeBonis, and May families, for their patience; Ken and Christine Kawasaki, Audrey Ness, K. Lynn Savage, Dr. Barbara Robson, Erica Hagen, Mary Johnson, Dianne Walker, and Michelle Noullet, for encouragement, support, and good ideas; Helen Munch, for keen editing; and all ESL teachers working with refugees in the camps and at home, for caring.

Printed in the United States of America

10   9   8   7   6   5   4   3

ISBN 0-13-612367-8

Prentice-Hall International (UK) Limited, *London*
Prentice-Hall of Australia Pty. Limited, *Sydney*
Prentice-Hall Canada Inc., *Toronto*
Prentice-Hall Hispanoamericana, S.A., *Mexico*
Prentice-Hall of India Private Limited, *New Delhi*
Prentice-Hall of Japan, Inc., *Tokyo*
Simon & Schuster Asia Pte. Ltd., *Signapore*
Editora Prentice-Hall do Brasil, Ltda., *Rio de Janeiro*

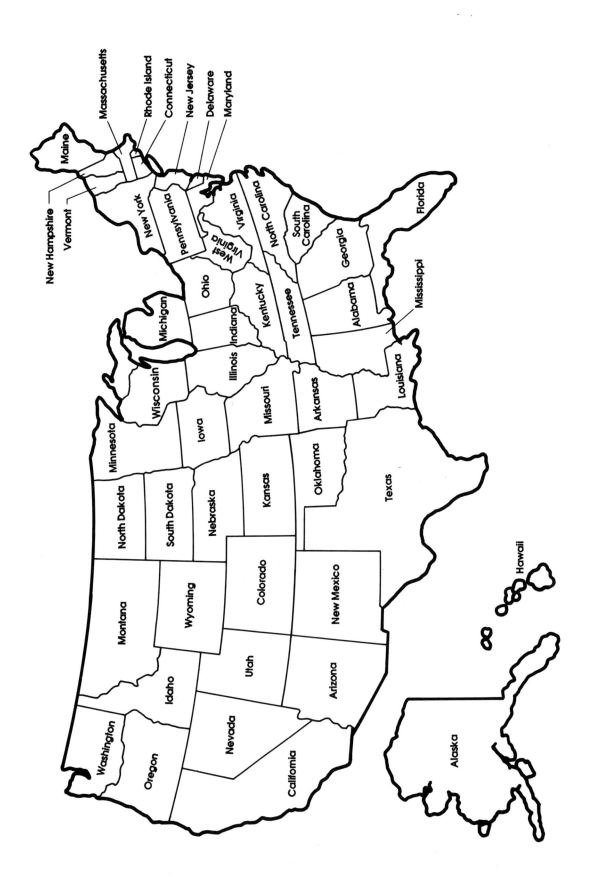

Contents

Part 1
The New Arrival

The New Arrival

Now I live in America. I'm living with a Laotian family in a small house. There are four rooms in our house. There's only one bedroom and one bathroom. There are ten people living in the house. It's crowded, but it's better than camp. This house is bigger than my house in camp.

I live in Boston. It's a big city. It's bigger than the city of Vientiane in Laos. There's a lot of traffic in Boston. It's a noisy city. It's confusing to go from one place to another. I get lost all the time.

Sometimes I miss the rice fields of Laos. I miss my small village and my family. When I think of them, I feel homesick.

There are many things that I like about Boston. I like to go to the movies. I like to go to the library, too. There are so many books there. There are a lot of things to learn. In my village there was just one school. Boston has many schools. I want to study in one of them. I'd like to study English again.

There are lots of cheap restaurants here. You can eat many different kinds of food. I don't like American food, but there are some Chinese restaurants that I like. I'd rather eat Chinese food than American food.

When I really feel lonely, I go to the park. I like the trees and flowers there. I also like to watch the birds. The park is my favorite place because it reminds me of my country.

Vocabulary

America(n)
Laos / Laotian
bedroom
bathroom
Boston / Vientiane
traffic
movies
library
school(s)
restaurants
park
trees
flowers
birds
lots of
kinds of

cheap
favorite
noisy
confusing
better than

because

miss(es)
can
watch(es)

get(s) lost
feel(s) homesick, lonely
I'd rather
remind(s) (me) of

True / False / Maybe

Write **T** if the answer is true,
      F if the answer is false,
      M if the answer is maybe.

1. ———— Sitha lives in America.

2. ———— Sitha lives alone.

3. ———— Boston is bigger than Vientiane.

4. ———— Sitha will study English again.

5. ———— Sitha usually feels lonely and homesick.

Understanding the Story

Write answers to the questions below. Use complete sentences.
Follow the example.

    Example: Where does Sitha live now?   *He lives in America.* _____

1. How many people live with Sitha? _____

   _____

2. In what city does Sitha live? _____

3. What does Sitha miss? _____

   _____

4. What does Sitha like about Boston? _____

   _____

5. What kind of food does Sitha like to eat? _____

   _____

Grammar

A. Study the adjectives and their comparative forms below.
Then complete each sentence with the correct comparative form.

big-bigger   **good-better**   **fast-faster**
small-smaller   **noisy-noisier**

1. My house is <u>big</u>. Your house is _____ than mine.

2. My city is <u>small</u>. Your city is _____ than mine.

3. The Mekhong River is <u>fast</u>. The Charles River is _____ than the Mekhong.

4. He's a <u>good</u> football player. You're a _____ football player than he is.

5. Boston is a <u>noisy</u> city. New York is a _____ city than Boston is.

B. Read the paragraph below. Then fill in each blank with the word *younger* or *older*.

I'm twenty years old. My sister is thirteen. My brother is twenty-five.
My sister's name is Mary. My brother's name is Henry.

1. Mary is my _____ sister.

2. Henry is my _____ brother.

3. Mary is _____ than Henry.

4. Henry is _____ than I am.

5. I am _____ than my sister.

Tell Me

Describe Boston. _____

_____

_____

_____

Describe your city. _____

_____

_____

_____

What do you like or not like about your city? _____

_____

_____

_____

Write a Description

Where do you like to go when you feel lonely or you want to be alone? Describe that place.

Different Customs

American customs are different from Laotian customs. There are many things that I find strange and confusing.

In America, I often see men and women holding hands. Sometimes I even see them kiss! In Laos we don't do such things in public.

Americans also dress differently. Sometimes the women wear shorts and sleeveless blouses. Laotian women are too shy to dress this way.

Americans move quickly. Everyone is busy and in a hurry. People often speak in loud voices. In Laos, life is slow and quiet. Maybe that's better; I don't know.

Laotians don't usually move far from their families. In America, that's not true. Young American men and women often leave their parents' home at age seventeen or eighteen.

Americans sometimes touch each other on the head. In Asia, people never do that. It would be rude.

Sometimes I don't understand what's happening around me. I can't believe what I see. Maybe this feeling is what they call "culture shock."

I can't decide which culture is better—mine or American. I hope things become less confusing. I must try to understand this new country.

Vocabulary

customs
such things
shorts
blouses
Asia(ns)
culture shock

different from
holding hands
sleeveless
shy
busy
loud
slow
quiet
true
rude

differently
in public
quickly
in a hurry

kiss(es)
dress(es)
wear(s)
move(s)
touch(es)
can't
decide(s)

True / False / Maybe

Write **T** if the answer is true,
      F if the answer is false,
      M if the answer is maybe.

1. _____ Lao culture is different from American culture.

2. _____ Laotian women wear shorts.

3. _____ Americans often speak loudly.

4. _____ Some Americans don't move far from their families.

5. _____ Most new arrivals have culture shock.

Understanding the Story

Write answers to the questions below. Use complete sentences.
Follow the example.

Example: What things are confusing to Sitha? *American customs are confusing to Sitha.*

1. What does Sitha see American men and women doing in public? _____

   _____

2. What do some American women wear? _____

   _____

3. How do Americans move? _____

4. What do young American men and women do? _____

   _____

5. What do Americans do that Asians think is rude? _____

   _____

Grammar

A. <u>Underline</u> the correct verb in each sentence below.

1. People (dress, wear) differently in America.

2. Women (dress, wear) shorts.

3. Lao women are too shy to (dress, wear) sleeveless blouses.

4. I like to (dress, wear) shorts.

5. In America, people (dress, wear) any way they want.

B. Match each <u>underlined</u> word with its opposite from the list below and fill in the blanks.

loud   **rude**   **shy**
slowly   **short**

1. They like to move <u>quickly</u>. We move _____ .

2. Life is <u>quiet</u> in Laos, but in America it's _____ .

3. Americans seem open and <u>friendly</u>. Laotians sometimes feel

_____ .

4. We try to be <u>nice and polite</u>, but sometimes we meet people who are

_____ .

5. We prefer to wear <u>long</u> pants. Some Americans like to wear

_____ pants.

Tell Me

Describe Lao customs. _____

_____

_____

_____

Describe your customs. _____

_____

_____

_____

Write a Letter

You are writing to a friend in your country. Tell him or her how you feel about America.

_____
(Place)

_____
(Date)

Dear _____ ,

Here I am in America. There are many things that I like. But some things are

strange and confusing. For example, _____

_____

_____

_____

_____

Your friend,

_____
(Your name)

When I was a small child, I was never lonely. My family was always around. My friends and I were together a lot. We were happy. Life was never boring. There was always a lot to do. No one was ever too busy to talk to you. I was happy to have such good friends.

Here in America, I often feel homesick. I think of my friends back in Laos. Sometimes it's lonely living in a foreign country. There are many young people living in my neighborhood, but I don't know any of them. The Laotian family that I live with is wonderful, but I need to make my own friends. Sometimes I feel depressed.

I miss my friends in Laos. I miss Lee Pao and Chue Vue. Think of the things we did together. Lee Pao and I played soccer. I don't see many people playing soccer in my neighborhood. I will have to learn some American games like football and baseball. When I have some American friends, I'll ask them to teach me.

Everyone needs friends. Everyone needs someone to talk to. I want to make new friends here in America. I hope I can make some friends soon.

Vocabulary

child
friends
life
neighborhood
Lee Pao
Chue Vue
soccer
games
football
baseball

happy
boring
foreign
wonderful
own
depressed
too busy

(n)ever

learn(s)
teach(es)
need(s)

True / False / Maybe

Write **T** if the answer is true,
      F if the answer is false,
      M if the answer is maybe.

1. _____ Sitha was never lonely in Laos.

2. _____ Sitha has many friends in America.

3. _____ Sometimes Sitha is depressed.

4. _____ Sitha can play baseball.

5. _____ Many people live in Sitha's neighborhood.

Understanding the Story

Write answers to the questions below. Use complete sentences.
Follow the example.

Example: Does Sitha feel homesick? _*Yes, he does.*_____

1. Why was Sitha happy when he was a small child? _____

_____

2. Why does he feel lonely in America? _____

_____

3. With whom does Sitha live now? _____

_____

4. What American games does Sitha want to learn? _____

_____

5. What does Sitha hope? _____

_____

Grammar

A. Look at the words below. Then read the story and fill in each blank with an appropriate word.

need(s)   **want(s)**   **would like**

I have many friends. Everyone (1)_____ friends. I'm bored with

some of my friends. I (2) _____ to make new friends. I

(3)_____ to make friends with people from foreign countries.

I don't have children. I (4) _____ to have children. Some people

feel unhappy if they don't have children. Not me. I don't (5) _____

children to be happy.

B. Use your own words to complete the sentences below.
Follow the example.

Example: When I have some American friends, *I will learn to play baseball.*

1. When I feel lonely, I _____

    _____

2. I am happy when _____

    _____

3. I feel depressed when _____

    _____

4. I feel wonderful when _____

    _____

5. It's boring when _____

    _____

Tell Me

What games did you play in your country? ———————————————————

———

———

———

What games do you play now, in America? ———————————————————

———

———

———

Buying Food

In Laos, I lived on a farm. I worked in the rice fields. My family and I had a big garden in back of our house. We grew tomatoes, cabbages, cucumbers, onions, and parsley in our garden. We had to work hard, but we were happy because we worked together.

Here in Boston, I can't grow rice. I have to buy it. Boston is a big city and there aren't any rice fields here. Rice is sold in supermarkets and in grocery stores.

I shop at the big supermarket in my neighborhood. It's around the corner from my house. The supermarket has many aisles. There are different things in each aisle. Some things are in plastic bags. Others are in boxes. I can never find the rice.

Things like coffee come in jars and cans. The measurements are different, too. In Laos, we use kilos and grams. In America, food is sold by the pound and ounces.

In the supermarket, tomatoes and cucumbers are wrapped in plastic. They look different from the foods we grew in our garden in Laos.

It's confusing to shop in the supermarket.

Vocabulary
farm
rice fields
garden
tomatoes
cabbages
cucumbers
onions
parsley
supermarkets
grocery stores
aisles
plastic bags
boxes
coffee
jars
cans
measurements
kilos / grams
pounds / ounces
wrapped
in back of
grew
sold
shop

True / False / Maybe

Write **T** if the answer is true,
     F if the answer is false,
     M if the answer is maybe.

1. _____ In Laos, Sitha had a rice field in back of his house.

2. _____ Sitha grows rice in Boston.

3. _____ There is a supermarket in Sitha's neighborhood.

4. _____ It's hard to find things in the supermarket.

5. _____ In the supermarket, the tomatoes are cheap.

Understanding the Story

Write answers to the questions below. Use complete sentences.
Follow the example.

Example: Can Sitha find the rice? _No, he can't._____

1. What did Sitha grow in his garden in Laos? _____

   _____

2. Why can't Sitha grow rice in Boston? _____

   _____

3. In the supermarkets, what does coffee come in? _____

   _____

4. What measurements are used in America? _____

   _____

5. How are the tomatoes and cucumbers wrapped? _____

   _____

Grammar

A. Study the past tense forms of the verbs below.
Then rewrite each sentence in the past tense.

live / lived	**sell / sold**	**has / had**
work / worked	**grow / grew**	

1. I live in Laos. _____

2. We grow tomatoes. _____

3. He has a garden. _____

4. They work hard. _____

5. She sells cucumbers. _____

B. Look at the list of items below. How is each one packaged
and sold in your supermarket? Follow the example.

ITEM	PACKAGED	SOLD
1. sugar	in a box or a bag	by the pound
2. apples	_____	_____
3. soap	_____	_____
4. bananas	_____	_____
5. noodles	_____	_____
6. toothpaste	_____	_____
7. rice	_____	_____
8. tea	_____	_____
9. milk	_____	_____
10. cooking oil	_____	_____

Finish the Dialog

Work with a partner or a small group to finish the dialog below.

Shopper: Where can I find sugar?

Clerk: In aisle 3.

Shopper: Can I find salt there, too?

Clerk:

Calling a Friend

In Laos, I lived in a very small village. My friend, Lek, lived in Vientiane, the capital of Laos. Vientiane was very far from my village.

One day my cousin decided to get married. I wanted to invite Lek to the wedding, but there weren't any telephones in my village. So, I wrote Lek a letter. I asked him to come to my village for the wedding. I mailed the letter at the post office.

On the day of the wedding, I waited for Lek to arrive. I waited a long time, but he never came. The wedding was very beautiful. Everyone had a lot of fun, but I was sad because Lek never came.

Two weeks later, I finally got a letter from Lek. He wrote that he didn't receive my letter until two days after the wedding! Mail was very slow in Laos. Sometimes it even got lost.

Now Lek lives in California. In America, most people have telephones. It's usually easy to get in touch with people by phone. One night I decided to telephone Lek. Here's what happened.

(The phone is ringing.) *Ring-ring-ring*

Man: Hello?
Sitha: Hello, is Lek there?
Man: You have the wrong number.
Sitha: Sorry. I'll try again.
(Sitha dials again.) *Ring-ring-ring*
Man: Hello?
Sitha: May I please speak to Lek?
Man: Didn't you just call?
Sitha: Well, uh, maybe.
Man: Listen, you have the wrong number. Look up the right number in the phone book.
Sitha: Excuse me, I won't call you again.

Vocabulary

Lek
capital
cousin
wedding
telephones / phone
letter
post office
California
wrong number

beautiful
sad
easy / easier

finally
until

write(s)
write / wrote
mailed
waited
arrive(s)
receive(s)
dial(s)
ring(s)

to get married
I'm tired of
get(s) in touch with
look(s) up

May I please speak to...?
I'd like to speak to...,
    please.
Stop bothering me!
Why don't you...?

(Sitha dials very carefully.) *Ring-ring-ring*

Man: Hello!

Sitha: I'd like to speak to Lek, please.

Man: Listen, you, I'm tired of answering the phone! You have the wrong number! Now stop bothering me!

Sitha: Excuse me, I'm sorry. I just came to this country. I'm trying to get in touch with one of my friends. He lives in California.

Man: Well, why don't you ask the operator to help you?

Sitha: Thank you, but I think I'll just write my friend a letter. It's easier.

True / False / Maybe

Write **T** if the answer is true,
    F if the answer is false,
    M if the answer is maybe.

1. ——— Vientiane is the capital of Thailand.

2. ——— Sitha mailed the letter at the post office.

3. ——— Sitha's letter got lost.

4. ——— Everyone in America has a phone.

5. ——— Sitha dialed the wrong number.

Understanding the Story

Write answers to the questions below. Use complete sentences.
Follow the example.

Example: Who is Lek? *He is Sitha's friend.*

1. Whom was Sitha phoning? _____

_____

2. Who answered the phone? _____

_____

3. How many times did Sitha try to telephone his friend? _____

_____

4. What was the problem? _____

_____

5. What did Sitha decide to do? _____

_____

Grammar

Study the past tense forms of the verbs below. Then rewrite each
sentence in the past tense.

lose / lost   **aren't / weren't**   **get / got**
write / wrote   **has to / had to**

1. I write to my friend Lek. _____

2. There aren't any phones in Sitha's village. _____

_____

3. The post office loses some letters. _____

_____

4. He has to call his cousin. _____

5. He gets the wrong number. _____

_____

Tell Me

Study the chart below. Then answer the questions.

HOURS	DAYS OF THE WEEK							
A.M. / P.M.	MON.	TUES.	WEDS.	THURS.	FRI.	SAT.	SUN.	
8 A.M.–5 P.M.	XXX	XXX	XXX	XXX	XXX	000	000	R
								A
5 P.M.–11 P.M.	***	***	***	***	***	000	000	T
								E
11 P.M.–8 A.M.	000	000	000	000	000	000	000	S

XXX = highest rates   *** = middle rates   000 = lowest rates

1. At what times and on what days are phone rates the highest?

   _____

2. At what times and on what days are phone rates the lowest?

   _____

Telephone Information

Study the information below. Then complete each sentence with the correct words or number.

DIAL	FOR
911	Emergencies (police, fire, ambulance)
800	Toll-free calls (Example: 800-432-5000)
Area Code	Long distance calls (Example: Area code 415-727-3695)
Directory Assistance	Information about telephone numbers, phone listings
Operator	Assistance with phone use, telephone problems, some emergencies

1. Call_____ if you can't find a telephone number.

2. Dial_____ if there's an emergency.

3. Ask for the_____ if you have trouble with your telephone.

4. An _____ number means you don't have to pay for the call.

5. When you telephone long distance, be sure to add the _____.

Part 2

Work and School

It's time for me to look for a job. In Laos, I was a farmer. I liked being a farmer. I like to work outdoors. I also like animals. So, farming was a perfect occupation for me.

I'd like to get an interesting job in America. There are many ways to look for a job. One way is to look in the newspaper. Newspapers advertise jobs in the classified section. You can find out what jobs are available in the "Want Ads" there.

This morning I bought a newspaper. It was full of job advertisements. "It must be easy to get a job," I thought. Here are some of the ads that were in the newspaper.

Wanted: Mechanic to repair cars. Call Ace Garage: 321-4567 after 5 P.M.

Wanted: Messengers for downtown office area. No experience necessary. Call 567-9810 from 1 to 4 P.M.

Wanted: Dishwashers for large restaurant. Call Hal at 234-8756.

I dialed the first number.

Man: Ace Garage. This is Tom.
Sitha: Hello. I'm calling about the mechanic job advertised in today's paper.
Tom: Do you have experience repairing cars?
Sitha: No, I don't.
Tom: Sorry. We want someone with experience.

"Well," I thought, "I might as well try again." I dialed the second number.

Woman: Good afternoon. Express Delivery, Wanda speaking.
Sitha: Hello. I'm calling regarding the messenger job.
Wanda: Can you drive a car?
Sitha: No, I can't.
Wanda: Sorry. We need someone who can drive.

Vocabulary

job
animals
farming
occupation
way(s)
newspaper
classified section
advertisements / ads
mechanic
cars
garage
messengers
experience
office area
dishwashers
restaurant
worker
interview
tomorrow
address

perfect
interesting
available
downtown
necessary
sharp

outdoors

thought
look(s) for / in
find(s) out
repair(ing)
drive(s)
calling about

might as well
regarding

Hold on...

"Maybe it isn't so easy to get a job," I thought. I tried the third number.

Woman: Hello. Hal's Hamburgers.
Sitha: I'd like to speak to Hal, please.
Woman: Is this about a job?
Sitha: Yes, it is.
Woman: What's your name?
Sitha: My name is Sitha Aedavang.
Woman: Hold on. I'll see if Hal is in.
Hal: Hello, Hal speaking.
Sitha: I'm calling about the dishwasher job.
Hal: Do you have any experience?
Sitha: No, but I can learn. I need a job and I'm a hard worker.
Hal: Okay. Come on in for an interview tomorrow at 9 A.M. sharp. The address is 28 White Street.
Sitha: Thank you. I'll see you tomorrow at 9 A.M.

True / False / Maybe

Write **T** if the answer is true,
        F if the answer is false,
        M if the answer is maybe.

1. _____ Sitha was a mechanic in Laos.

2. _____ Sitha likes to work outdoors.

3. _____ Sitha drives a car.

4. _____ Sitha has experience as a messenger.

5. _____ Sitha will get a job as a dishwasher.

Understanding the Story

Write answers to the questions below. Use complete sentences.
Follow the example.

Example: Does Sitha know how to drive? *No, he doesn't.*

1. Where in the newspaper does Sitha find job ads? _____

_____

2. How many phone calls does Sitha make? _____

_____

3. What does a mechanic need to know? _____

_____

4. What does a messenger need to know? _____

_____

5. Which job will Sitha interview for? _____

_____

Grammar

Study the past tense forms of the verbs below. Then rewrite each
sentence in the past tense.

tell / told	buy/bought	speak / spoke	is / was
think / thought	hold / held	answer(ed)	

1. I buy a newspaper from the man on the corner. _____

_____

2. I speak to a woman on the phone. _____

_____

3. She tells me to "Hold on." _____

4. I hold on until a man answers. _____

_____

5. I think getting a job is easy. _____

Tell Me

Describe your occupation in your country. _____

_____

_____

_____

Describe your occupation in America. _____

_____

_____

_____

Reading the Want Ads

Read the newspaper want ads below. Then work with a partner
or a group to answer these questions about each ad:

- What job is this ad for?

- What do the abbreviations mean? (rm., Biling., reqd., and so on)

- What do you need to know?

- How can you find out more?

BABYSITTER NEEDED—Spanish-speaking in exchange for rm. and board. 556-9543.

HANDYMAN (M / F)—For office bldg. Exper. required. Excel. benefits. Call Martin 649-8687.

P / T SEC'Y—Accntg. firm. 20 hr. pwk. Computer skills preferred. Gd. salary. Call 557-2980.

TEACHER AIDE—Biling. class. Secondary credential reqd. Call 655-3900.

CAFETERIA WRKR—P / T public sch. No exper. nec. Call 557-3322.

OFFICE HELP—Gd. phone, some typg, add. mach. F / T 665-8702.

The Interview

My interview is at 9 A.M. I leave the house at 8 A.M. I have to take a bus across town. I don't want to be late for my first appointment. I have the address of the restaurant, but I'm not sure where the restaurant is. I don't have much experience in getting around the city. I hope I don't get lost. I'm nervous. This is my first job interview.

At the restaurant

Hostess: Good morning, may I help you?
Sitha: Yes. I have an appointment with Hal.
Hostess: Is this about a job?
Sitha: Yes, it is.
Hostess: You're a half hour late.
Sitha: I'm sorry. I got lost. I took the wrong bus.
Hostess: Hal won't like that. I'll see if he can speak with you now. Have a seat, please.

In Hal's office

Hal: Hello. My name's Hal Greene.
Sitha: How do you do? I'm Sitha Aedavang.
Hal: Yes. Your appointment was for 9 o'clock. You're late.
Sitha: I'm very sorry. I got lost. I'm new in this city. It's difficult for me to find my way.
Hal: If I give you a job here, you can't be late.
Sitha: Yes, I understand.
Hal: How did you find out about this job?
Sitha: I saw your ad in the newspaper.
Hal: Do you have any restaurant experience?
Sitha: No, I don't, but I'd like to learn.
Hal: What's your occupation?
Sitha: I was a farmer in my country.

Vocabulary

appointment
Aedavang
Hal Greene
education
application form

nervous

across town
a half hour late

leave(s)

take(s) a bus
getting around
find(s) out about
fill(s) out
look(s) over
keep(s) on hand
come(s) up
give(s) someone a call

Have a seat, please.
How do you do?
You're late.
Sorry

Hal: A farmer? Where are you from?
Sitha: I'm from Laos.
Hal: How much education do you have?
Sitha: Not much. You see, in my country...
Hal: Okay, okay. Fill out this application form.

Later. Hal looks over Sitha's application.

Hal: Sorry, son, there's nothing available right now.
        I'll keep your application on hand. If anything
        comes up, I'll give you a call.
Sitha: Thank you. Good-bye.

True / False / Maybe

Write **T** if the answer is true,
       F if the answer is false,
       M if the answer is maybe.

1. _____ It's Sitha's first job interview.

2. _____ He wants a job as a waiter.

3. _____ Sitha took the wrong bus.

4. _____ Sitha's friend told him about the job.

5. _____ Hal will give Sitha a call.

Understanding the Story

Write answers to the questions below. Use complete sentences. Follow the example.

Example: How late was Sitha? *He was a half hour late.*

1. Why was Sitha nervous? _____

    _____

2. At what time was his appointment? _____

    _____

3. Why was Sitha late? _____

    _____

4. Was Hal angry at Sitha for being late? _____

5. What did Hal say he would do? _____

    _____

Grammar

Complete each sentence with a verb phrase from the list below.

fill out	**find out about**	**keep on hand**
looked over	**comes up**	

1. "How did you _____ this job?" asked Hal.

2. He told him to _____ an application form.

3. Hal _____ Sitha's application.

4. "If anything _____ ," said Hal, "I'll give you a call."

5. Hal said he would _____ Sitha's application _____.

Tell Me

What are some questions you might ask at a job interview? _____

_____

_____

_____

What questions might the interviewer ask you? _____

_____

_____

_____

I wasn't having much luck with the newspaper job ads. So, one morning I decided to try the state employment office. I dressed carefully and took a bus downtown. This time I didn't get lost. When I got to the office, I had to wait in line for a half hour. Finally, it was my turn. A woman told me to take a seat. Her name was Ms. Lopez. She was very polite. I had to fill out a form. She looked the form over and then asked me some questions.

Ms. Lopez:	Where are you from?
Sitha:	I'm from Laos.
Ms. Lopez:	What was your occupation there?
Sitha:	I was a farmer.
Ms. Lopez:	Are you employed now?
Sitha:	No, I'm not, but I'd like to be.
Ms. Lopez:	How much education do you have?
Sitha:	Not much, only a few years of elementary school.
Ms. Lopez:	What kind of job are you looking for?
Sitha:	It doesn't matter. I just want a job.
Ms. Lopez:	Do you have experience in anything in particular?
Sitha:	I can do many things well, but the only job I ever had was in farming.
Ms. Lopez:	Are you interested in job training?
Sitha:	Yes. I'd like that.
Ms. Lopez:	Can you work nights?
Sitha:	Yes, I can.
Ms. Lopez:	Are you married?
Sitha:	No, not yet.
Ms. Lopez:	Do you have a social security number?
Sitha:	No, I don't. What is that?

Vocabulary

luck
state employment office
Ms. Lopez
my turn
elementary school
job training
social security number
social security
   administration
files

polite
carefully
employed
interested in

wait(s) in line
take(s) a seat

anything in particular

It doesn't matter.
You're welcome.

Ms. Lopez: You will need to get one from the social
security administration before you start to
work.

Sitha: Okay, I'll do that.

Ms. Lopez: Let me see. I don't have anything in my files
for you now. If anything comes up, I'll give
you a call. Is this your home phone number?

Sitha: Yes, it is. Thank you very much.

Ms. Lopez: You're welcome. Good-bye.

True / False / Maybe

Write **T** if the answer is true,
   F if the answer is false,
   M if the answer is maybe.

1. _____ Sitha went to the social security administration.

2. _____ He had to fill out a form.

3. _____ The form was difficult to understand.

4. _____ Sitha has a social security number.

5. _____ Ms. Lopez will find Sitha a job.

Understanding the Story

Write answers to the questions below. Use complete sentences.
Follow the example.

Example: Where was the employment office?   *It was downtown.* _____

1. Why did Sitha go to the state employment office? _____

_____

2. How long did he have to wait in line? _____

_____

3. What are some of the questions Ms. Lopez asked Sitha? _____

_____

4. Where can Sitha get a social security number? _____

_____

5. What kind of education does Sitha have? _____

_____

Grammar

Connect the sentences using *but*. Follow the example.

Example: I don't have a job. I'd like one. *I don't have a job, but I'd like one.*

1. I'm not employed. I'd like to be. _____

_____

2. I don't have much experience. I can learn. _____

_____

3. I can do many things. In Laos, I worked as a farmer. _____

_____

4. I'm not married. I'd like to be. _____

_____

5. I don't have a social security number. I'll get one. _____

_____

Finish the Dialog

Work with a partner or a small group to finish the dialog below.

Interviewer: Did you fill out the application form?
Sitha: Yes, I did, but what is a social security number?

Interviewer:

Fill Out the Application

Work alone or with a small group to fill out the application form below.
If you need help, ask your teacher.

APPLICATION FOR EMPLOYMENT
(Please Print)

Date_____ Job(s) Applied for: _____

Personal

Name_____ Telephone _____
      Last   First   Middle

Address _____
       Number   Street   City   State   ZIP

Are you over 18 years of age?_____ Social Security Number _____

Are you legally eligible for employment in the United States? _____

Education

Last School Attended _____
                 Name   Address

Circle Last Year Completed: 1   2   3   4   5   6   7   8   9   10   11   12   13   14   15   16

Special Training / Skills / Licenses: _____

Experience

List your employers, starting with the last one first.

Period Employed	Name and Address	Job	Salary
From: To:			
From: To:			
From: To:			

Are there any other experiences, skills, or qualifications that you feel will help you perform the job

for which you are applying?_____ If you answered "yes," please explain: _____

_____

References

Do not list relatives or former employers.

Name	Address	Occupation	Years Known

Applicant's Signature _____

I always read the newspaper. It helps me improve my English. I come across interesting advertisements all the time. Today I found this one.

English as a Second Language (ESL) classes to be held at Charles River Junior College: Mon.–Fri., 9 A.M. to 3 P.M., starting Jan. 11. Classes are free of charge. Register between Jan. 4–10 at the college: 14 River St., Boston.

The last time I studied English was in Ban-Vi-Nai refugee camp. I think it would be good if I studied again. I need the practice. I can study during the day because I don't have a job yet.

I walked to Charles River Junior College to register. It wasn't far from my house. I went to the registrar's office. I had to wait in a long line. There were people from many different countries waiting in line, too. They spoke their native languages. When it was my turn, I filled out an application form. In America, I am always waiting in lines and filling out forms!

Vocabulary

junior college
ESL
Ban-Vi-Nai
refugee camp
practice
registrar's office
native languages

free of charge
during the day

improve(s)
register(s)

come(s) across

True / False / Maybe

Write **T** if the answer is true,
   F if the answer is false,
   M if the answer is maybe.

1. _____ Sitha never reads the newspaper.

2. _____ Sitha studied English in the refugee camp.

3. _____ The English classes are held Mondays and Fridays only.

4. _____ The classes are expensive.

5. _____ Sitha is a good student.

Understanding the Story

Write answers to the questions below. Use complete sentences.
Follow the example.

Example: Is the college near Sitha's house? *Yes, it is.* _____

1. Where will the ESL classes be held? _____

   _____

2. What is the address of the college? _____

   _____

3. At what time are classes held? _____

   _____

4. What date do classes begin? _____

   _____

5. When should Sitha register? _____

   _____

Grammar

A. Complete each sentence with an expression from the list below.

> **come across**   **my turn**   **during the day**
> **free of charge**   **all the time**

1. He likes to read the newspaper. He reads it _____.

2. You don't have to pay for the classes. They're _____.

3. When it was _____, I registered for my classes.

4. If you _____ a good job ad, let me know.

5. _____ I can study English.

B. Connect the sentences below using *because*. Follow the example.

> *Example:*   I want to get a job. I need the money.
> *I want to get a job because I need the money.*

1. I always read the newspaper. I learn a lot of English from it. _____

    _____

2. I think I'll take an English class. I need the practice. _____

    _____

3. I can study during the day. I don't have a job yet. _____

    _____

4. I can walk to the college. It isn't far from my house. _____

    _____

5. I had to wait in line. There were many people in the registrar's office. _____

    _____

Tell Me

Describe school and your classes in your country. _____

_____

_____

_____

Describe school and your classes in the U.S. _____

_____

_____

_____

Let's Write

Write about why you are studying English now.

Student Days

There are about 25 students in my English class. They come from many different countries. About five students are from Cuba. There are three Vietnamese and eight Cambodians. There are students from Hong Kong and Taiwan. They speak Chinese. There are also some Russian, Haitian, and Salvadoran students.

I come from Laos. There are many ethnic groups in Laos. My ethnic group is Lao. There's another student from Laos in my class. Her ethnic group is Hmong. She speaks Hmong, but she can't speak Lao at all. We come from the same country, but we can't speak to each other. Isn't that strange?

I was so surprised and happy to find out that one of my classmates is Nguyen Van Cuong. I know him from Phanat Nikhom transit center in Thailand. We traveled to America on the same plane. I asked Cuong about Sary, our Cambodian friend. He said that he sees Sary now and then. Cuong asked me to come over for dinner. I said okay. It'll be nice to see his family again.

Everyone in my class is a foreigner. Everyone is very friendly. We like to practice English with each other. It's a good idea to speak English all the time. After all, practice makes perfect.

My teacher is a middle-aged American woman. She's about forty-five years old. She has blue eyes and blonde hair. She's an attractive lady. She's older than my teacher was in the refugee camp, but she's very friendly.

Vocabulary
Cuba
Vietnam
Hong Kong / Chinese
ethnic groups
Taiwan / Chinese
Russia(ns)
Haiti(ans)
El Salvador
Salvadorans
Hmong / Laotians
classmates
Nguyen Van Cuong
Phanat Nikhom
transit center
Thailand
Sary
foreigners
surprised
middle-aged
blonde
attractive
friendly
now and then
traveled
practice makes perfect

True / False / Maybe

Write **T** if the answer is true,
       F if the answer is false,
       M if the answer is maybe.

1. ———— There are 25 students in Sitha's English class.

2. ———— Some students are from Africa.

3. ———— The Hmong speak Lao.

4. ———— Cuong is from Thailand.

5. ———— Sitha's teacher is married.

Understanding the Story

Write answers to the questions below. Use complete sentences.
Follow the example.

Example: What language does Sitha speak? *He speaks Lao.* _____

1. What countries do Sitha's classmates come from?_____

    _____

2. Why does the other student from Laos speak another language? _____

    _____

3. Where did Sitha meet Cuong? _____

    _____

4. Where is Sary from? _____

5. How old is Sitha's teacher? _____

Grammar

Rewrite the sentences below using *there is* or *there are*. Follow the example.

> *Example:*   Many refugees are studying English.
> *There are many refugees studying English.*

1. Many students are in my class. _____

   _____

2. The students are from different countries. _____

   _____

3. One student is from Cuba. _____

   _____

4. Another student is from Laos. _____

   _____

5. Some Russians, Haitians, and Salvadorans are in the class. _____

   _____

Tell Me

Describe Sitha's classmates. _____

_____

_____

_____

Describe your classmates. _____

_____

_____

_____

Finish the Dialog

Work with a partner or a small group to finish the dialog below.

Sam: Where are you from?
Chan: I'm from Cambodia.
Sam: Cambodia? Where's that?

Chan:

It took me about 20 minutes to walk to Nguyen Van Cuong's place. His apartment is very small, but very clean.

Cuong spoke to me while his wife cooked dinner. "There are some things here that I can't get used to," he said. "In Vietnam, my family depended on me. Here, I can hardly speak English. Everyone depends on my sixteen-year-old daughter, Tran. She speaks English well. We depend on her to answer the telephone, to do the shopping, and to speak to the doctor. I even depend on her to call my boss when I'm sick. I'm afraid she will forget her Vietnamese customs. Sometimes I feel ashamed. Is it right for a father to depend on his daughter?"

Cuong's wife cooked a delicious dinner. For the first time ever, I ate Vietnamese food. We had Còm (rice), Canh Chua (sweet and sour soup), Ca' Chiên (fried fish), Thịt Kho (beef stew), and Dô Xāo (vegetables). I ate a lot and felt very full.

Cuong's daughter, Tran, arrived late. She was wearing tight jeans and a T-shirt. Her hair was cut short and she wore a lot of makeup. She looked quite different from the Tran I remembered. Cuong seemed very unhappy. "Look at my daughter," he said. "She is becoming more American every day. Soon she will forget how to speak Vietnamese."

Tran looked at me and spoke. "You know, Sitha," she said, "now that we live in a new country, we have to change a little to fit in. I won't forget my own traditions, but I must also adapt to American life. I can't just be the same in America as I was in Vietnam. Don't you agree?"

I didn't know what to say. I felt confused. I feel bad for Cuong, but I also understand his daughter. What advice can I give them?

Vocabulary

minutes
apartment
boss
Tran
tight jeans
T-shirt
makeup
traditions
advice

clean
delicious

hardly

cooked
ate

is becoming
get(s) used to
depend(s) on
look(s) at
fit(s) in
adapt(s) to
feel(s) ashamed
feel(s) bad for

I'm afraid that
Don't you agree?

True / False / Maybe

Write **T** if the answer is true,
        F if the answer is false,
        M if the answer is maybe.

1. _____ Sitha took a bus to Cuong's place.

2. _____ Cuong depends on his wife for help.

3. _____ Tran speaks English well.

4. _____ Tran is more American than Vietnamese.

5. _____ Tran will forget how to speak Vietnamese.

Understanding the Story

Write answers to the questions below. Use complete sentences. Follow the example.

Example: How old is Tran?   *She is sixteen years old.* _____

1. What did Cuong's wife do while Cuong spoke to Sitha? _____

_____

2. Why is Cuong unhappy? _____

_____

3. What did Sitha eat for dinner? _____

_____

4. What was Tran wearing? _____

_____

5. What does Tran tell Sitha? _____

_____

Grammar

A. Complete each sentence with a verb phrase from the list below.

get used to   **adapt to**   **fit in**
depends on   **agrees with**

1. In America, Cuong _____ his daughter for many things.

2. Tran wants to change so she can _____ .

3. Sitha _____ both Cuong and Tran.

4. Cuong finds it hard to _____ American life.

5. He can't _____ many things.

B. Rewrite the sentences below using the past continuous—
WAS / WERE + verb – *ing*. Follow the example.

    Example: She wore tight jeans. *She was wearing tight jeans.*

1. Cuong spoke to Sitha. _____

2. Cuong's wife cooked dinner. _____

3. They ate Vietnamese food. _____

4. Tran became more American every day. _____

    _____

5. Sitha felt confused. _____

Tell Me

What advice would you give Cuong? _____

_____

_____

_____

What advice would you give Tran? _____

_____

_____

_____

What things do you depend on others to do for you? _____

_____

_____

_____

Part 3

Life in America

12

A New Schedule

I study English every day. My class starts at 9 A.M. I always get up early, at about 6:30 A.M., and eat breakfast. I usually have rice, pork, and eggs. I prefer Lao food to American food. After breakfast, I wash up and get ready for school.

This morning I got a phone call. It was from Ms. Lopez at the employment office. There's a job opening for me. It's a janitor's job. I'll have to work nights. My hours are from 6 P.M. until midnight. I can start tomorrow. I'm lucky. I can go to school during the day and work at night. It'll be nice to earn some money.

Now I'm very busy. Here is my new schedule.

6:30 A.M.	get up, eat breakfast, get ready for school
9 A.M.–3 P.M.	school
6 P.M.–midnight	work

Vocabulary

breakfast
pork
eggs
job opening
janitor
midnight
schedule

prefer(s)

get(s) up
wash(es) up
get(s) ready for
earn(s) money

True / False / Maybe

Write **T** if the answer is true,
      F if the answer is false,
      M if the answer is maybe.

1. _____ Sitha gets up at 9 A.M.

2. _____ Sitha got a phone call from the restaurant.

3. _____ Sitha does his homework in the afternoon.

4. _____ His job hours are 6 P.M. to 12 A.M.

5. _____ Sitha likes to be busy.

Understanding the Story

Write answers to the questions below. Use complete sentences.
Follow the example.

Example: What kind of job did Sitha get? _He got a janitor's job._

1. What does Sitha eat for breakfast? _____

_____

2. Who called Sitha from the employment office? _____

_____

3. What hours is Sitha in school? _____

4. What hours does Sitha work? _____

5. Why does Sitha say he's lucky? _____

_____

Grammar

Connect the sentences below using *after*. Follow the example.

> *Example:*   He gets home. Then he goes to bed.
> *After he gets home, he goes to bed.*

1. I get up. Then I eat breakfast. _____

   _____

2. I eat breakfast. Then I wash up. _____

   _____

3. I wash up. Then I get ready for school. _____

   _____

4. I get to school. Then I study all day. _____

   _____

5. I get home from school. I go to my job. _____

   _____

Tell Me

What was your schedule in your country? _____

_____

_____

_____

How would you like to spend your time every day? _____

_____

_____

_____

Comparing Schedules

Write answers to the questions below. Then ask a classmate
the same questions and compare your answers.

1. When do you get up every morning?

    You _____

    Classmate _____

2. What do you eat for breakfast?

    You _____

    Classmate _____

3. What do you do after breakfast?

    You _____

    Classmate _____

4. What do you eat for lunch?

    You _____

    Classmate _____

5. What do you do in your free time?

    You _____

    Classmate _____

6. Where do you work or study?

    You _____

    Classmate _____

7. How do you get to work or to school?

    You _____

    Classmate _____

13

My New Job

I'm a janitor in a local high school. I work with two other men. One man is from El Salvador and the other is from Hong Kong. The Salvadoran man is a refugee, like me. His name is Carlos. The man from Hong Kong is an immigrant. His name is Lin Fong. None of us can speak English very well, but we all practice with each other.

My boss is American. His name is Joe Smith. He speaks very quickly. Sometimes he gets angry when we don't understand him. I'm not afraid of him. I just ask him to speak slowly. When he's not angry, he's very nice. Sometimes he even jokes with us.

At 7:30 every night, we get a dinner break. My boss goes to a restaurant to eat. I want to save money, so I bring my dinner from home. Carlos and Lin Fong do, too. For dinner I usually eat rice, vegetables, and pork. Lin Fong eats rice and pork, too. Carlos eats chicken and rice for dinner. Joe always tells us what he ate in the restaurant. He usually has soup, steak, potatoes, and a salad. I'm used to eating a lot of rice. I really don't like potatoes.

Lin Fong, Carlos, and I are good friends. Lin Fong wants us to meet his family. He's married and has three children. Carlos is single like me. On Sunday, Carlos and I will go to Lin Fong's house for lunch. It's nice to have friends.

Vocabulary

high school
Carlos
immigrant
Lin Fong
Joe Smith
dinner break
chicken
soup
steak
potatoes
salad
lunch

local

get(s) angry
be afraid of
joke(s) with
be used to

True / False / Maybe

Write **T** if the answer is true,
      F if the answer is false,
      M if the answer is maybe.

1. _____ Sitha works in a local restaurant.

2. _____ The two other men are both immigrants.

3. _____ Sitha is afraid of his boss.

4. _____ The men take a one-hour dinner break.

5. _____ On Sunday, Sitha will visit Lin Fong and his family.

Understanding the Story

Write answers to the questions below. Use complete sentences.
Follow the example.

Example: What is the name of Sitha's boss? *His name is Joe Smith.* _____

1. Who are the two men who work with Sitha? _____

_____

2. What does Sitha do when he can't understand his boss? _____

_____

3. What does Joe Smith usually eat for dinner? _____

_____

4. How many children does Lin Fong have? _____

_____

5. What will Sitha and Carlos do on Sunday? _____

_____

Grammar

Rewrite the sentences below using BE USED TO + verb – *ing*.
Follow the example.

     Example: I study in the morning.   *I'm used to studying in the morning.*

1. He works in the evening. _____

   _____

2. They eat rice for dinner. _____

   _____

3. She doesn't eat lunch. _____

   _____

4. We get a dinner break at 7:30 P.M. _____

   _____

5. Joe eats dinner in a restaurant. _____

   _____

Tell Me

Describe Sitha's boss. _____

_____

_____

_____

Describe your boss (if you have one). _____

_____

_____

_____

What do you usually eat for dinner? _____

_____

_____

Let's Write

Write about the things you're used to doing.

14

Meeting Sary

Yesterday when I got on the bus, someone called my name. It was Sary, my Cambodian friend from Phanat Nikhom transit center.

"Sary," I said, "you look so different. I think you gained weight."

"Yes," he said, laughing, "the food in Boston is much better than the food in Phanat Nikhom."

Sary told me that he was working in a factory during the day and studying electronics and English at night. "I'll stay in the factory for another year or so," he said, "until I finish school. Then I'll have a skill and I can look for a better job."

Sary's words made me think about my future. Should I be studying a skill?

Sary also told me another interesting thing. "You know, I'm going out with Cuong's daughter, Tran. At first, some of my Cambodian friends were angry. They said that I should not go out with a Vietnamese. But I think that here in America, we are all the same. We should forget our differences. What do you think, Sitha?"

People are always asking me what I think, it seems. I'm so mixed up that I don't know what I think anymore. What do you think?

Vocabulary

factory
electronics
skill
future

all the same

gained weight
think(s) about
going out with
be mixed up

What do you think?

True / False / Maybe

Write **T** if the answer is true,
      F if the answer is false,
      M if the answer is maybe.

1. ———— Sary is Vietnamese.

2. ———— Sary works in a factory.

3. ———— Sitha is studying a skill.

4. ———— Sitha is going out with Tran.

5. ———— Sitha feels mixed up.

Understanding the Story

Write answers to the questions below. Use complete sentences.
Follow the example.

Example: Who called Sitha's name on the bus? ___*Sary did.*___

1. How did Sary look? _____

_____

2. What does Sary do during the day and at night? _____

_____

3. What did Sitha begin to think about? _____

_____

4. What did Sary's friends say about going out with Tran?_____

_____

5. What do people always ask Sitha? _____

_____

Grammar

A. Complete each sentence with a verb phrase from the list below.

get mixed up   **go out with**   **think about**
gain weight   **get on**

1. If you eat ice cream every day, you will _____ .

2. Her parents don't want her to _____ him.

3. When I'm busy, I don't _____ my problems.

4. Sometimes when I study my English lessons, I _____ .

5. Sary saw me _____ the bus.

B. Use your own words to complete each sentence below. Follow the example.

Example: I think that *Sary is learning a skill—English.*

1. He thinks that _____

_____

2. He told me that _____

3. She said that _____

4. You know that _____

5. I'm so mixed up that _____

Tell Me

What are three reasons for studying a skill? _____

_____

_____

_____

What are three skills you would like to study? _____

_____

_____

_____

Let's Write

Write about your future. What do you think about it?

15

The Robbery

I was coming back from work. It was after midnight. I was waiting for a bus on the corner of 28th Street. There wasn't anyone else around. Suddenly, a man came over to me. He was very tall. He had brown hair, a beard and a mustache, and brown eyes. He looked around, then asked, "Do you have a match?"

"Sure," I said, and I gave him a book of matches. All of a sudden, he took out a gun and said, "Give me all your money."

I was so nervous that I didn't know what to do. I couldn't think in English, so I started to speak Lao. The man said, "Hey man, I don't understand any Spanish. Just give me the money." I was really scared then. I gave him all my money and he ran away quickly.

I wasn't sure what to do next. Should I run after the man? Should I try to catch him? Should I call for help? I felt so alone.

Just then, a young couple walked by. I said to them, "Somebody just robbed me." The couple told me to go to the police station. They showed me where it was. Luckily, it was just around the corner.

Vocabulary

robbery
beard
mustache
match(es)
gun
Spanish
couple
police station

anyone else
somebody

suddenly
all of a sudden
just then
luckily

catch(es)
robbed

come(s) back from
come(s) over
looked around
took out
run(s) / ran away
run(s) after

True / False / Maybe

Write **T** if the answer is true,
   F if the answer is false,
   M if the answer is maybe.

1. _____ Sitha was waiting for a friend.

2. _____ The man asked Sitha for the time.

3. _____ The man was nervous.

4. _____ The man thought Sitha was Cuban.

5. _____ The couple told Sitha where the police station was.

Understanding the Story

Write answers to the questions below. Use complete sentences.
Follow the example.

   Example: What did the man ask Sitha for first?   *He asked him for a match.*

1. What time was it when Sitha was robbed? _____

   _____

2. Where was Sitha at that time? _____

   _____

3. What did the man look like? _____

   _____

4. What did the man take from Sitha? _____

   _____

5. How did Sitha feel? _____

   _____

Grammar

A. Complete each sentence with a word or phrase from the list below.

suddenly   **just then**   **luckily**
all of a sudden   **then**

1. First we had dinner, _____ we went out.

2. _____ it began to rain.

3. _____ I had my umbrella with me.

4. _____ I looked up and saw the moon.

5. It rained for a few minutes, then _____ it stopped.

B. Complete each sentence with a verb phrase from the list below.

looked around   **took out**   **walked by**
come back   **come over**

1. I _____ for my friend, but I didn't see him.

2. The man _____ a gun.

3. What time do you _____ from work?

4. On my way to work, I _____ the school.

5. Can you _____ for dinner tonight?

Tell Me

What should you do if somebody robs you? _____

_____

_____

_____

What should you do if you go out alone at night? _____

_____

_____

_____

Finish the Dialog

Work with a partner or a small group to finish the dialog below.

Woman: Help! Help!
Man walking by: What's the matter?
Woman: Someone took my handbag!

Man:

16

At the Police Station

There were many people waiting at the police station. The officers were very busy. The phones were ringing, and there was a lot of noise and confusion. I looked around for someone to help me.

A lady waiting to see an officer complained loudly. "These cops don't pay attention to anyone. I've waited here one hour already! They just tell me to be patient and wait my turn."

I also had to wait and wait and wait. Finally, an officer called me.

Officer: Your name?
Sitha: Sitha Aedavang.
Officer: What's the problem?
Sitha: Someone stole my money.
Officer: How much money did you lose?
Sitha: $30.
Officer: Can you describe the person?
Sitha: Yes, I can. It was a man...
Officer: That's okay. Fill out this form. Be sure to give all the details: the time, the date, and the place of the robbery. Make your description of the person as accurate as possible.
Sitha: I'll try. It was pretty dark and it's difficult to remember everything.
Officer: We'll do our best to find the person, but don't count on it.
Sitha: It sure is dangerous to be out alone at night.
Officer: You're lucky you only lost some money and not your life!

Vocabulary

officers
noise
confusion
lady
cops
person
details
description

exact
as accurate as possible
pretty dark

loudly
already

complained
describe
remember

look(s) around for
pay(s) attention to
be patient
wait my turn
be sure to
do our best

Don't count on it.

True / False / Maybe

Write **T** if the answer is true,
   F if the answer is false,
   M if the answer is maybe.

1. ———— The police station was busy.

2. ———— The lady was angry.

3. ———— Sitha had to wait a long time.

4. ———— Sitha could not describe the man.

5. ———— The police will find the man.

Understanding the Story

Write answers to the questions below. Use complete sentences.
Follow the example.

Example: How much money did Sitha lose? _He lost $30._____

1. What was happening at the police station? _____

   _____

2. What did the lady complain about? _____

   _____

3. What details should Sitha give the police? _____

   _____

4. Why might Sitha have difficulty with the details? _____

   _____

5. Why does the officer think that Sitha is "lucky"? _____

   _____

Grammar

A. Rewrite each sentence below using the present perfect tense—
HAVE / HAS + verb – *ed*. Follow the example.

> *Example:*   We complained to the police.
> *We have complained to the police.*

1. I waited for one hour. _____

2. Someone robbed me! _____

3. They described the person. _____

4. The police looked for the man. _____

5. She remembered all the details. _____

B. Complete each sentence with a verb phrase from the list below.

> **be patient   pay attention to   count on it**
> **do our best   wait your turn**

1. I tried to see the officer first, but the lady said to me, "_____

    _____."

2. We _____ to arrive in class on time.

3. The officer said, "We might get your money back, but don't

    _____ ."

4. It's hard to _____ sometimes.

5. He didn't _____ the advice of his friends.

Tell Me

What happens to people who steal in your country? _____

_____

_____

_____

Were you ever robbed? What happened? _____

_____

_____

_____

17

Buying Clothes

It's almost winter. It's getting cold. I'm not used to cold weather, but I hope I'll get used to it. I'm looking forward to seeing snow. I've never seen snow before. In Laos, it never snows. I'm from the lowlands. We have a warm climate in the lowlands.

I have to buy some winter clothes. I need a winter coat, sweaters, heavy pants, gloves, a scarf, and a hat. Clothes are expensive and I don't have a lot of money. I'll have to buy things little by little.

Today I'm going shopping at the department store. There's a sale on wool sweaters. I don't know what size I take. I hope the salesperson will help me.

At the department store

Information Clerk:	May I help you?
Sitha:	Yes. Where's the men's department?
Clerk:	It's on the third floor. Take the escalator over there.

On the third floor

Sitha:	Is this the men's department?
Salesclerk:	No, it isn't. The men's department is behind the shoe department to your right.
Salesclerk:	Can I help you?
Sitha:	Yes. I want to buy a sweater.
Salesclerk:	What size do you wear?
Sitha:	I'm not sure. A small size.
Salesclerk:	Yes, you Cuban people are small.
Sitha:	I'm not Cuban. I'm from Laos. Laotians are small people, too.
Salesclerk:	Here's a size 34. Try it on.
Sitha:	It fits, but I don't like the color. Do you have green?

Vocabulary

snow
lowlands
warm climate
clothes
winter coat
wool sweaters
heavy pants
gloves
scarf
hat
department store
sale
size
salesperson
information clerk
escalator
salesclerk
color

cold
expensive

little by little

fit(s)

look(s) forward to
try(ies) it on
have (has) in stock

I'm not sure.

Salesclerk: No, this is the only color we have in stock.
Why don't you try the boy's department on
the second floor. They might also have your
size.

Sitha: Thank you. That's a good idea.

True / False / Maybe

Write **T** if the answer is true,
F if the answer is false,
M if the answer is maybe.

1. _____ Sitha is used to snow.

2. _____ The wool sweaters are on sale.

3. _____ The salesclerk is a woman.

4. _____ Sitha wears a size 34.

5. _____ The boy's department is on the third floor.

Understanding the Story

Write answers to the questions below. Use complete sentences.
Follow the example.

Example: What is Sitha looking forward to? *He's looking forward to seeing snow.*

1. What clothes does Sitha have to buy?_____

_____

2. Why will he buy his clothes little by little? _____

_____

3. What is on sale at the department store? _____

_____

4. Where does the salesclerk think Sitha is from? _____

_____

5. Why doesn't Sitha want the size 34 sweater he tried on? _____

_____

Grammar

Complete each sentence with a phrase from the list below.

little by little	**try on**	**on sale**
have in stock	**look forward to**	

1. Sitha's going to the department store because the sweaters there are

    _____ .

2. I _____ buying some new clothes.

3. _____ she's learning about American sizes.

4. We had to _____ many shoes before we found some
   we liked.

5. What color coats do they _____ ?

Comparing Sizes

Fill in the chart below with information about sizes.
If you need help, ask your teacher or another classmate.

CLOTHING	SIZES in your country	SIZES in America
1. coat	_____	_____
2. sweater	_____	_____
3. long pants	_____	_____
4. shirt or blouse	_____	_____
5. shoes	_____	_____
6. gloves	_____	_____

Tell Me

How do men and women dress in your country? _____

_____

_____

_____

What is your favorite article of clothing? Why? _____

_____

_____

_____

Finish the Dialog

Work with a partner or a small group to finish the dialog below.

Salesclerk: May I help you?
Customer: Yes. I'm looking for a coat.

Salesclerk:

18

Money

I didn't buy anything in the department store. On my way home, I saw a nice-looking green sweater in the window of a small clothing store. I went in and tried the sweater on. It fit very well, and it wasn't too expensive. The price on the tag was $15.99. I took the sweater to the cashier. She asked me for $17.11.

"But the price is $15.99," I said.

"You must pay 7% sales tax here," she said. "The total is $17.11."

I always get mixed up when I use American money. American paper money is called dollars. In Laos, money is called *kip*. Each American dollar bill is worth 100 cents. There are coins, also. Each coin has a different value. A penny is 1 cent, a nickel is 5 cents, a dime is 10 cents, a quarter is 25 cents, and a half-dollar is 50 cents. It's very confusing.

I gave the cashier three five-dollar bills, two ones, two dimes, and one penny. She took the money and counted it. Then she gave me back one dime. "You gave me too much," she said. Two dimes and one penny are 21 cents, not 11 cents. Be careful with your money. Someone else might cheat you."

I always get my dimes and nickels mixed up. A dime is smaller than a nickel, but it's worth more. I hope I don't make that mistake again. Next time the cashier may not be so honest.

Vocabulary

window
clothing store
price
tag
cashier
sales tax
total
dollars/cents
dollar bill
coins
value

7 percent = 7%
dollar = 100 cents (100¢)
half-dollar = 50 cents (50¢)
quarter = 25 cents (25¢)
dime = 10 cents (10¢)
nickel = 5 cents (5¢)
penny = 1 cent (1¢)

nice-looking
honest

counted
is worth
cheat (s)

get(s) mixed up
give(s) back
make(s) a mistake
be careful with

True / False / Maybe

Write **T** if the answer is true,
   F if the answer is false,
   M if the answer is maybe.

1. _____ The price of the sweater was $15.99.

2. _____ Sitha gave the cashier too much money.

3. _____ The cashier gave Sitha back a quarter.

4. _____ A nickel is worth more than a dime.

5. _____ Sitha made the same mistake again.

Understanding the Story

Write answers to the questions below. Use complete sentences.
Follow the example.

Example: What did Sitha want to buy? *He wanted to buy a sweater.* _____

1. Why did Sitha pay $17.11 for the sweater? _____

   _____

2. How much money did Sitha give the cashier? _____

   _____

3. What did the cashier tell Sitha to do? _____

   _____

4. What two coins does Sitha get mixed up? _____

   _____

5. What may happen to Sitha "next time"? _____

   _____

Grammar

Complete the sentences using comparatives from the list below.

smaller   less   more
bigger   heavier

1. A dime is worth _____ than a nickel.

2. A quarter is _____ than a penny.

3. A half-dollar is _____ than a quarter.

4. A nickel is worth _____ than a dime.

5. A penny is _____ than a half-dollar.

How Much Do You Have?

Work with a partner or a small group to solve the problems below.

1. You have 3 dimes, 2 quarters, and 1 nickel. How much money do you have?

   _____

2. You gave the cashier a one-dollar bill for a 35¢ newspaper. How much money

   should you get back? _____

3. The operator said to put 60¢ into the pay telephone. What 3 coins could you use?

   _____

4. The price of the book is $15.95 and 5% sales tax. What is the total amount you must

   pay? _____

5. You have $1.98 in your hand—1 dollar bill, 3 quarters, 1 dime, 1 nickel, and the rest

   are pennies. How many pennies do you have? _____

Money Review

Write the names of American coins and their values below.
Then answer the questions.

COIN	VALUE
penny	*one cent (1¢)*
_____	_____
_____	_____
_____	_____
_____	_____

1. How many pennies are in one dollar? _____

2. How many nickels are in one dollar? _____

3. How many dimes are in one dollar? _____

4. How many quarters are in one dollar? _____

5. How many half-dollars are in one dollar? _____

Part 4

My Greatest
Accomplishment

19

Apartment Hunting

I live with a Laotian family in a small house. It's very crowded. I'd like to move out and rent an apartment, but I don't want to live alone. Carlos, my Salvadoran friend, is also looking for an apartment. Maybe we can live together as roommates. It's expensive to live in the city. I hope I can find a cheap apartment to rent.

I read the apartment ads in the newspaper. The rents are high. Some real estate agencies advertise apartments for rent. I went to an agency in my neighborhood. The realtor said he could find me an apartment, but I have to pay him. I don't know if it's worth it. How do I know that he's honest? Can I count on him?

I hope I find an apartment soon. I'm looking forward to living in my own place.

Vocabulary

house
apartment
roommates
apartment ads
rents
real estate agencies
realtor

rent(s)

move(s) out
could find
count on

it's worth it

True / False / Maybe

Write **T** if the answer is true,
  F if the answer is false,
  M if the answer is maybe.

1. _____ Sitha lives in an apartment.

2. _____ He wants to live alone.

3. _____ Carlos will be his roommate.

4. _____ Real estate agencies advertise apartments.

5. _____ The realtor is an honest man.

Understanding the Story

Write answers to the questions below. Use complete sentences.
Follow the example.

   Example: Where is Carlos from? *He's from El Salvador.*

1. Why does Sitha want to move? _____

   _____

2. Why does he want a roommate? _____

   _____

3. Where does Sitha find apartment ads?_____

   _____

4. Who can help him find an apartment? _____

   _____

5. What is Sitha looking forward to? _____

   _____

Grammar

Rewrite the sentences below by changing the <u>underlined</u> verb into a participle—VERB + *ing*. Follow the example.

Example: There are many people. They <u>live</u> in the house.

There are many people living in the house.

1. There are many people. They <u>live</u> alone. _____

   _____

2. I see them. They <u>read</u> the newspaper. _____

   _____

3. There are real estate agencies. They <u>advertise</u> apartments. _____

   _____

4. There's a realtor in my neighborhood. He <u>helps</u> me. _____

   _____

5. He has a problem. He can't <u>find</u> a roommate. _____

   _____

Tell Me

Where do people live in your country? (in apartments? in houses? other?) _____

_____

_____

_____

Who makes a good roommate? _____

_____

_____

_____

Finish the Dialog

Work with a partner or a small group to finish the dialog below.

Sitha: I found a nice apartment for rent. Would you like to go see it?
Carlos: Well, I don't know. Tell me about it first.

Sitha:

Reading Apartment Ads

Work with a partner or a small group to answer the questions about each of the ads below.

- How many rooms does the apartment have?

- What do the abbreviations mean? (unf., nr., Gd.)

- Is it furnished or unfurnished?

- Do you have to pay a deposit?

- Whom should you call about the apartment?

$550 Sunny unf. 1 BR w/AEK; nu paint.
Call Capp Realty, 565-4875.

$850 4 rms. w/DR; WBF in LR. Deposit req.
Anderson Realty, 665-3232.

$375 unf. studio. No pets.
Call 665-4600.

$450 furn. studio nr downtown. Gd transport.
Call 695-3300, Pat.

$875 2 BR nr lake; prkg. garage. Lease.
Mgr. 695-2202.

$400 garden apt. nr college; sublet May thru Aug.
Joe. 655-6959.

There are many apartment buildings in my neighborhood. I pass them on my way to school. Today I saw a sign outside one building. It said Apartments for Rent. Inquire Within. I went inside and spoke to the superintendent, Mr. Patel. He was from India. He showed me an apartment on the fifth floor. It had one bedroom, a kitchen, a living room, and a bathroom. There wasn't any furniture, but there was a stove and a refrigerator. The bathroom had a leaking faucet. I asked Mr. Patel about the apartment.

Sitha:	How much is the rent?
Mr. Patel:	It's $550 a month and a cleaning deposit.
Sitha:	That's a lot of money for me.
Mr. Patel:	We'll paint the apartment for you and fix the broken faucet.
Sitha:	That's still a lot of money. Do you have anything cheaper?
Mr. Patel:	There's a cheaper apartment downstairs, on the ground floor.
Sitha:	I'd like to see that one.

The ground floor apartment had one small bedroom, a kitchen as part of the living and dining area, and a tiny bathroom with a shower only. There were two chairs and a couch in the living area.

Mr. Patel:	The rent here is $475 a month. There's a one-year lease and a $100 cleaning deposit.
Sitha:	I'll have to talk to my friend first. He wants to share the apartment with me. He'll want to see it, too.
Mr. Patel:	Okay, think it over. It doesn't matter to me. Lots of people want apartments these days.

Vocabulary

apartment buildings
sign
superintendent
India(n)
Mr. Patel
furniture
stove
refrigerator
leaking faucet
cleaning deposit
downstairs
ground floor
shower
one-year lease
chairs
couch

broken
cheaper
tiny

outside

fix(es)
paint(s)
share(s)
think(s) it over

It doesn't matter
Inquire Within

True / False / Maybe

Write **T** if the answer is true,
      F if the answer is false,
      M if the answer is maybe.

1. _____ Sitha looked at a ground floor apartment.

2. _____ The first apartment had furniture.

3. _____ The superintendent will paint the apartment.

4. _____ The second apartment rented for $550 a month.

5. _____ Sitha will rent the second apartment.

Understanding the Story

Write answers to the questions below. Use complete sentences.
Follow the example.

    Example: What is the superintendent's name? *His name is Mr. Patel.*

1. Where did Sitha see the Apartment for Rent sign? _____

   _____

2. To whom did Sitha speak about the apartments? _____

   _____

3. What was inside the first apartment? _____

   _____

4. What did the superintendent say he would fix? _____

   _____

5. What did Sitha say he wanted to do? _____

   _____

Grammar

<u>Underline</u> the correct adjective in each sentence below.

1. There wasn't (some, any) furniture in the first apartment.

2. I'll need to buy (some, any) furniture.

3. There were (some, any) chairs in the second apartment.

4. I don't have (some, any) money to pay the realtor.

5. We didn't have to pay (some, any) cleaning deposit for our apartment.

Furnishing an Apartment

Work with a partner or a small group to complete the chart below. You have just rented an unfurnished apartment. You need some furniture and supplies. What do you need for each room?

ROOM	FURNITURE / SUPPLIES
1. living room	_____
	_____
	_____
2. kitchen	_____
	_____
	_____
	_____
3. bedroom	_____
	_____
	_____
4. bathroom	_____
	_____
	_____

Write a Description

Describe a favorite room in your house or apartment.

21

Meeting the Neighbors

Carlos and I are now sharing a ground floor apartment. We're happy living there. Carlos is a good roommate. He's honest, neat, and clean. We get along well together. Carlos has a lot of friends. They often stop in and visit us. We bought some used furniture: a table, four chairs, and a lamp. I always look forward to coming back to my new home.

The other day when I came home, I met my neighbor. Her name is Susan. She stopped to speak to me in the hall.

Susan: Hi! Do you live in this building?
Sitha: Yes, I do.
Susan: I don't think I've seen you before.
Sitha: Well, I only moved in last month.
Susan: Oh. Do you live with anyone?
Sitha: Yes, I do. I live with my friend Carlos. We work together. Do you live here, too?
Susan: Yes. I live alone.
Sitha: Don't you get lonely sometimes?
Susan: Sometimes. Would you like to come in and see my place?
Sitha: Well, okay.

Susan: Sit down. I'll make some coffee.
Sitha: Thank you. You have a nice apartment.
Susan: I used to live here with my husband. He fixed up the place. Now we're divorced. Are you married?
Sitha: No, but I'd like to get married.
Susan: Do you have a girlfriend?
Sitha: I used to have one, but I don't now.

Susan: What do you do?
Sitha: I'm a janitor.
Susan: I'm a secretary. I hate my job. I'd like to go back to school to become a nurse.

Vocabulary

used furniture
table
lamp
Susan
neighbor
husband
girlfriend
secretary
nurse
theater
world
weekend

neat
divorced

someday

hate(s)

stop(s) in
moved in
come(s) in
sit(s) down
fixed up
go(es) back
get along well together

Sitha: I'm studying English now. I'd like to go to college
           someday.
Susan: Your English is pretty good. Do you watch TV a
           lot or go to the movies?
Sitha: We don't have a TV and I don't have much time
           for the movies. I read the newspaper a lot.
Susan: Maybe we could go to a movie together
           sometime. There's a good theater in the
           neighborhood. It shows movies from all over the
           world. We could go on a weekend.
Sitha: I'm not sure about that. I'll have to think it over.
Susan: Sure. We could ask your roommate, too.

True / False / Maybe

Write **T** if the answer is true,
     F if the answer is false,
     M if the answer is maybe.

1. _____ Carlos and Sitha are roommates.

2. _____ Carlos doesn't have any friends.

3. _____ Sitha and Carlos bought new furniture.

4. _____ Susan is married.

5. _____ Sitha will go to the movies with Susan.

Understanding the Story

Write answers to the questions below. Use complete sentences.
Follow the example.

Example: Why is Carlos a good roommate? *He's honest, neat, and clean.*

1. Where do Sitha and Carlos live? _____

_____

2. How long have they lived there? _____

_____

3. What is Susan's job? _____

4. What would Susan like to do? _____

_____

5. What does Susan tell Sitha about the neighborhood? _____

_____

Grammar

Sometimes people ask you a lot of questions.
You may not want to answer all of them. Read the questions below.
If you don't like answering a question, mark **X** under Personal;
if you don't mind answering, mark **X** under Not Personal.
Discuss your answers with the class.

Questions	Personal	Not Personal
1. How long have you lived here?	☐	☐
2. Do you live with anyone?	☐	☐
3. Are you married?	☐	☐
4. Do you have a girlfriend / boyfriend?	☐	☐
5. What do you do?	☐	☐

Tell Me

What are some questions you might ask someone you don't know well? _____

_____

_____

_____

What are some questions you would not ask anyone? _____

_____

_____

_____

22

My Neighborhood

Many people from all over the world live in my neighborhood. They speak different languages and some wear different clothes. I see them shopping in the stores nearby. There's an Italian delicatessen, a Chinese fish market, a Russian bakery, an Indian spice shop, and several small Asian grocery stores. There are also lots of restaurants. My neighborhood's a busy place and sometimes it gets noisy.

There's a park in my neighborhood, too. Sometimes I go there just to sit and watch the people. There's a playground, and many children go there to play on the slide and swings. People also come to walk their dogs and to talk to one another. One day while I was sitting on a bench, I heard two men talking to each other. The language they spoke sounded very beautiful to me. I asked them in English what language they were speaking. It was Italian and they tried to teach me a few words. I found out that they lived in the apartment building next to mine. We spoke in English for awhile and they invited me to visit them.

My neighborhood is an interesting place. Whenever I feel lonely, I walk around and listen to all the people speaking different languages. In America, I can watch people from all over the world living together.

Vocabulary

Italian
delicatessen

fish market
bakery
spice shop
playground
children
slide
swings
dogs
bench

beautiful

awhile

sounded
walk(s) around

True / False / Maybe

Write **T** if the answer is true,
  F if the answer is false,
  M if the answer is maybe.

1. _____ Sitha lives in a Southeast Asian neighborhood.

2. _____ There are no restaurants in the neighborhood.

3. _____ There is a park in the neighborhood.

4. _____ He met two men from India.

5. _____ The men spoke Italian.

Understanding the Story

Write answers to the questions below. Use complete sentences.
Follow the example.

Example: Where does Sitha live? _*He lives in an apartment building.*_____

1. What kind of stores are there in Sitha's neighborhood? _____

   _____

2. What else is in the neighborhood? _____

   _____

3. What does Sitha do in the park?_____

   _____

4. Why do people go to the park? _____

   _____

5. What did the two men invite Sitha to do? _____

   _____

Grammar

Use *while* to connect the first sentence to the second sentence. Follow the example.

    Example: I'm a student. I'm living at home.

                        While I'm a student, I'm living at home.

1. I was sitting on the bench. I watched the children playing. _____

   _____

2. Their mothers were watching. The children went down the slide. _____

   _____

3. I was walking around. I heard people speaking different languages. _____

   _____

4. I was listening to the people. I saw a dog. _____

   _____

5. The dog was running around. I was talking to my neighbors. _____

   _____

Tell Me

Describe Sitha's neighborhood. _____

_____

_____

_____

Describe your neighborhood. _____

_____

_____

_____

Let's Write

Write about one of your neighbors.

23

My Greatest Accomplishment

Today my English teacher asked each student to write a composition. The topic is My Greatest Accomplishment.

I'm not sure what to write. I've thought about the topic for a long time. I've done so many things in the past year. Leaving Laos and swimming across the Mekhong River were accomplishments. Coming to America, getting a job, going to school, and meeting new people were all accomplishments.

All in all, though, I think my greatest accomplishment was learning English. I still make many mistakes. Sometimes I don't understand everything people say, but each day I get better and better.

I told my teacher that the composition was difficult to write. After all, it's hard to measure everything you have done in your life!

Vocabulary
composition
topic
accomplishment
mistakes
better and better
all in all
measure

True / False / Maybe

Write **T** if the answer is true,
　　　 F if the answer is false,
　　　 M if the answer is maybe.

1. _____ Sitha's English teacher asked the students to read a story.

2. _____ Sitha did many things during the past year.

3. _____ Sitha still makes mistakes.

4. _____ Sitha's English is getting better.

5. _____ Sitha will write a good composition.

Understanding the Story

Write answers to the questions below. Use complete sentences.
Follow the example.

　　Example: What river did Sitha swim across? *It was the Mekhong River.*

1. What is the topic of Sitha's composition? _____

_____

2. What were some of Sitha's accomplishments? _____

_____

3. What does Sitha think his greatest accomplishment is? _____

_____

4. What did Sitha tell his teacher? _____

_____

5. Why did he say that? _____

_____

Grammar

A. Combine the sentences below. Change the first sentence into a gerund—
VERB + *ing*. Then make it the subject of the new sentence.
Follow the example.

>   *Example:*   I'm learning English. It's difficult.   *Learning English is difficult.*

1. I'm writing a composition. It isn't easy. _____

    _____

2. I left Laos. It was hard. _____

3. I swam across the Mekhong River. It made me tired. _____

    _____

4. I go to school. It makes me happy. _____

    _____

5. I meet new people every day. It's a great experience. _____

    _____

B. Study the past and present perfect tense forms of the verbs below.
Then rewrite each sentence in the present perfect tense.
Follow the example.

>   *Example:*   I wrote my composition.   *I have written my composition.*

>   **did-done**   **got-gotten**   **came-come**
>   **went-gone**   **saw-seen**

1. I did many things in my life. _____

    _____

2. I came a long way from home. _____

    _____

3. I got a job. _____

4. I saw many things. _____

5. I went many places. _____

Tell Me

What are some of your accomplishments? _____

_____

_____

_____

What do you think *your* greatest accomplishment is? _____

_____

_____

_____

Write Your Own Story

You have read many stories about Sitha and his life in Laos and in the United States of America. Now it's time for you to write your own story. Use the space below to make some notes. Then write your story on a separate sheet of paper.

Good luck!

Answer Key

Answer Key

1. The New Arrival

True/False/Maybe
1. T 2. F 3. T 4. M 5. F

Understanding the Story
1. Ten people live with Sitha. 2. He lives in Boston. 3. He misses the rice fields, his village, and his family. 4. He likes the movies and the library (and the trees, flowers, and birds in the park). 5. He likes to eat Chinese food.

Grammar
A. 1. bigger 2. smaller 3. faster 4. better 5. noisier

B. 1. younger 2. older 3. younger 4. older 5. older

2. Different Customs

True/False/Maybe
1. T 2. F 3. T 4. M 5. M

Understanding the Story
1. He sees them holding hands and kissing (in public).
2. They wear shorts and sleeveless blouses. 3. They move quickly. 4. They often leave their parents' home (at age 17 or 18). 5. They touch people on the head.

Grammar
A. 1. dress 2. wear 3. wear 4. wear 5. dress

B. 1. slowly 2. loud 3. shy 4. rude 5. short

3. Getting to Know People

True/False/Maybe
1. T 2. F 3. T 4. F 5. M

Understanding the Story
1. His family was always around. His friends and he were together a lot. 2. He doesn't know anyone. He doesn't have friends. 3. He lives with a Laotian family. 4. He wants to learn football and baseball. 5. He hopes that he can make some friends soon.

Grammar
A. 1. needs (wants or would like) 2. want (need or would like)
3. want (would like) 4. want (would like) 5. need

103

4. Buying Food
True/False/Maybe
1. F 2. F 3. T 4. T 5. M

Understanding the Story
1. He grew tomatoes, cucumbers, onions, and parsley. 2. There aren't any rice fields in Boston. 3. Coffee comes in cans (in the supermarket). 4. Pounds and ounces are used in America.
5. Tomatoes and cucumbers are wrapped in plastic.

Grammar
1. I lived in Laos. 2. We grew tomatoes. 3. He had a garden.
4. They worked hard. 5. She sold cucumbers.

5. Calling a Friend
True/False/Maybe
1. F 2. T 3. M 4. F 5. T

Understanding the Story
1. He was phoning his friend Lek. 2. A man answered the phone. 3. He tried to telephone (his friend) three times.
4. He got/had the wrong number. 5. He decided to write (his friend) a letter.

Grammar
A. 1. I wrote to my friend Lek. 2. There weren't any phones in Sitha's village. 3. The post office lost some letters. 4. He had to call his cousin. 5. He got the wrong number.

Telephone Information
1. Directory Assistance 2. 911 3. Operator 4. 800 5. Area Code

Tell Me
1. Monday to Friday from 8 A.M. to 5 P.M. 2. Saturday and Sunday all day, and Monday to Friday from 11 P.M. to 8 A.M.

6. Looking for a Job
True/False/Maybe
1. F 2. T 3. F 4. F 5. M

Understanding the Story
1. He finds job ads in the classified section. 2. He makes three phone calls. 3. A mechanic (S/He) needs to know how to repair cars. 4. A messenger (S/He) needs to know how to drive. 5. Sitha/He will interview for the dishwasher job.

Grammar
1. I bought a newspaper from the man on the corner. 2. I spoke to a woman on the phone. 3. She told me to "Hold on." 4. I held on until a man answered. 5. I thought getting a job was easy.

Reading the Want Ads

Here's what the abbreviations mean: rm.=room; biling.=bilingual; reqd.=required; sch.=school; nec.=necessary; add. mach.=adding machine; M/F=male or female; bldg.=building; exper.=experience; excel.=excellent; P/T=part time; F/T=full time; sec'y.=secretary; acctng.=accounting; hr.=hour; pwk.=per week; gd.=good; typg.=typing.

7. The Interview

True/False/Maybe

1. T **2.** F **3.** T **4.** F **5.** M

Understanding the Story

1. It was his first job interview. **2.** His appointment was for 9 A.M. **3.** He took the wrong bus. **4.** Yes, he was (angry). **5.** He said he would keep Sitha's application on hand (and give him a call if anything comes up).

Grammar

1. find out about **2.** fill out **3.** looked over **4.** comes up **5.** keep _____ on hand

8. At the Employment Office

True/False/Maybe

1. F **2.** T **3.** M **4.** F **5.** M

Understanding the Story

1. He wasn't having much luck with the newspaper job ads. **2.** He had to wait in line for half an hour. **3.** What was your occupation? Are you employed now? How much education do you have? What kind of job are you looking for? Do you have any experience in anything in particular? Are you interested in job training? Can you work nights? Are you married? Do you have a social security number? **4.** He can get a social security number from the social security administration. **5.** Sitha has only a few years of elementary school (for his education).

Grammar

1. I'm not employed, but I'd like to be. **2.** I don't have much experience, but I can learn. **3.** I can do many things, but in Laos I worked as a farmer. **4.** I'm not married, but I'd like to be. **5.** I don't have a social security number, but I'll get one.

9. English Classes

True/False/Maybe

1. F **2.** T **3.** F **4.** F **5.** M

Understanding the Story
1. They will be held at Charles River Junior College.   2. The address is 14 River Street, Boston.   3. The classes are held Monday through Friday from 8 A.M. to 2 P.M.   4. Classes begin on January 11.   5. He should register between January 4 and 10 (at the college).

Grammar
A. 1. all the time   2. free of charge   3. my turn   4. come across   5. During the day

B. 1. I always read the newspaper because I learn a lot of English from it.   2. I think I'll take an English class because I need the practice.   3. I can study during the day because I don't have a job yet.   4. I can walk to the college because it isn't far from my house.   5. I had to wait in line because there were many people in the registrar's office.

10. Student Days

True/False/Maybe
1. T   2. F   3. F   4. F   5. M

Understanding the Story
1. They come from Cuba, Vietnam, Cambodia, Hong Kong, Taiwan, Russia, Haiti, and El Salvador.   2. She is Hmong (a different ethnic group).   3. He met him at the transit center in Thailand.   4. Sary is from Cambodia.   5. She is middle-aged (about 45).

Grammar
1. There are many students in my class.   2. There are students from different countries.   3. There is one student from Cuba.
4. There is another student from Laos.   5. There are some Russians, Haitians, and Salvadorans in the class.

11. At Cuong's Place

True/False/Maybe
1. F   2. F   3. T   4. M (T)   5. M

Understanding the Story
1. She cooked dinner.   2. He is unhappy because his daughter/Tran is becoming more American every day.   3. He ate Vietnamese food (Com, Canh Chua, Ca Chien, Thit Kho, and Do Xao).   4. She was wearing tight jeans and a T-shirt (and a lot of makeup).   5. She tells him that she has to change to fit in, that she won't forget her customs, that she must adapt to American life.

Grammar
A. 1. depends on   **2.** fit in   **3.** agrees with   **4.** adapt to   **5.** get used to

B. 1. Cuong was speaking to Sitha.   **2.** Cuong's wife was cooking dinner.   **3.** They were eating Vietnamese food.
4. Tran was becoming more American every day.   **5.** Sitha was feeling confused.

12. A New Schedule

True/False/Maybe
1. F   **2.** F   **3.** M   **4.** T   **5.** M

Understanding the Story
1. He eats rice, pork, and eggs.   **2.** Ms. Lopez called (him).
3. He's in school from 9 A.M. until 3 P.M.   **4.** He works from 6 P.M. until midnight.   **5.** He says he's lucky because he can go to school during the day and work at night (and he can earn some money).

Grammar
1. After I get up, I eat breakfast.   **2.** After I eat breakfast, I wash up.   **3.** After I wash up, I get ready for school.   **4.** After I get to school, I study all day.   **5.** After I get home from school, I go to my job.

13. My New Job

True/False/Maybe
1. F   **2.** F   **3.** F   **4.** M   **5.** T

Understanding the Story
1. The two men are Carlos and Lin Fong.   **2.** He asks him to speak slowly.   **3.** He usually eats soup, steak, potatoes, and salad.   **4.** Lin Fong/He has three children.   **5.** They will go to Lin Fong's house for lunch.

Grammar
1. He's used to working in the evening.   **2.** They're used to eating rice for dinner.   **3.** She isn't used to eating lunch.
4. We're used to getting a dinner break at 7:30 P.M.   **5.** Joe's used to eating dinner in a restaurant.

14. Meeting Sary

True/False/Maybe
1. F   **2.** T   **3.** F   **4.** F   **5.** T

Understanding the Story
1. He looked different. (He looked like he gained weight.)
2. Sary works in a factory during the day and studies electronics at night.   **3.** He began to think about his future (and studying a skill).   **4.** They said he should not go out with a Vietnamese.
5. They always ask him what he thinks.

Grammar

A. 1. gain weight   2. go out with   3. think about   4. get
mixed up   5. get on

15. The Robbery

True/False/Maybe

1. F   2. F   3. M   4. T   5. T

Understanding the Story

1. It was after midnight.   2. He was on the corner of 28th
Street.   3. He had brown hair, a beard, a mustache, and brown
eyes.   4. He took his matches and all his money.
5. He felt (so) alone (nervous and scared).

Grammar

A. 1. then   2. All of a sudden (Suddenly)   3. Luckily   4. Just
then   5. suddenly (all of a sudden)

B. 1. looked around   2. took out   3. come back   4. walked by
5. come over

16. At the Police Station

True/False/Maybe

1. T   2. T   3. T   4. F   5. M

Understanding the Story

1. There were many people waiting. (It was crowded. The
officers were busy, the phone was ringing.)   2. She said the
cops didn't pay attention to anyone. (She waited one hour.
They told her to be patient and wait her turn.)   3. He should
give them the time, date, and place of the robbery.   4. It was
pretty dark and he might not remember all the details
(everything).   5. He only lost some money and not his life!

Grammar

A. 1. I have waited for one hour.   2. Someone has robbed me!
3. They have described the person.   4. The police have looked
for the man.   5. She has remembered all the details.

B. 1. Wait your turn   2. do our best   3. count on it   4. be
patient   5. pay attention to

17. Buying Clothes

True/False/Maybe

1. F   2. T   3. M   4. T   5. F

Understanding the Story

1. He needs a winter coat, sweaters, heavy pants, gloves, a
scarf, and a hat.   2. Clothes are expensive and he doesn't have
a lot of money.   3. Wool sweaters are on sale.   4. The
salesclerk (S/He) thinks he's from Cuba.   5. He doesn't like
the color.

Grammar
1. on sale **2.** look forward to **3.** Little by little **4.** try on
5. have in stock

18. Money
True/False/Maybe
1. T **2.** T **3.** F **4.** F **5.** M

Understanding the Story
1. He had to pay 7% sales tax. **2.** He gave her $17.21 (3 five-dollar bills, 2 ones, two dimes, and a penny.) **3.** She told him to be careful with his money. **4.** He gets nickels and dimes mixed up. **5.** Someone might cheat him.

Grammar
1. more **2.** bigger/heavier **3.** heavier/bigger **4.** less
5. smaller

How Much Do You Have?
1. 85¢ **2.** 65¢ **3.** 2 quarters and 1 dime **4.** $16.75
5. 8 pennies

Money Review
1. 100 **2.** 20 **3.** 10 **4.** 4 **5.** 2

19. Apartment Hunting
True/False/Maybe
1. F **2.** F **3.** M **4.** T **5.** M

Understanding the Story
1. It's very crowded in his house. **2.** He doesn't want to live alone. **3.** He finds them in the newspaper. **4.** A real estate agency/a realtor can help him (find an apartment). **5.** He is looking forward to living in his own place.

Grammar
1. There are many people living alone. **2.** I see them reading the newspaper. **3.** There are real estate agencies advertising apartments. **4.** There's a realtor in my neighborhood helping me. **5.** He has a problem finding a roommate.

Reading Apartment Ads
Here's what the abbreviations mean: unf.=unfurnished; w/=with; BR=bedroom; AEK=all electric kitchen; nu=new; furn.=furnished; nr=near; gd=good; transport.=transportation; rms.=rooms; DR=dining room; WBF=wood-burning fireplace; LR=living room; req.=required; prkg.=parking; mgr.=manager; thru=through.

20. Apartment for Rent
True/False/Maybe
1. T **2.** F **3.** T **4.** F **5.** M

Understanding the Story

1. He saw it outside an apartment building.   **2.** He spoke to the superintendent (Mr. Patel).   **3.** There was a stove and a refrigerator (one bedroom, a kitchen, a living room, and a bathroom).   **4.** He said he would fix the broken/leaking faucet.   **5.** He said he wanted to talk to his friend first.

Grammar

1. any **2.** some **3.** some **4.** any **5.** any

21. Meeting the Neighbors

True/False/Maybe

1. T **2.** F **3.** F **4.** F **5.** M

Understanding the Story

1. They live in a ground floor apartment.   **2.** They have lived there (about) one month.   **3.** She's a secretary.   **4.** She'd like to go back to school and become a nurse.   **5.** She says there's a good theater in the neighborhood (that shows movies from all over the world).

22. My Neighborhood

True/False/Maybe

1. F **2.** F **3.** T **4.** F **5.** T

Understanding the Story

1. There's a delicatessen, a fish market, a bakery, a spice shop, and several small grocery stores.   **2.** There are a lot of restaurants and a park (with a playground).   **3.** He sits and watches the people.   **4.** They go to play on the slide and swings, to walk their dogs, and to talk to one another.   **5.** They invited him to visit them.

Grammar

1. While I was sitting on the bench, I watched the children playing. OR I was sitting on the bench while I watched the child playing.   **2.** While their mothers were watching, the children went down the slide. OR Their mothers were watching while the children went down the slide.   **3.** While I was walking around, I heard people speaking different languages. **4.** While I was listening to the people, I saw a dog.   **5.** The dog was running around while I was talking to my neighbors. OR While the dog was running around, I was talking to my neighbors.

23. My Greatest Accomplishment

True/False/Maybe
1. F **2.** T **3.** T **4.** T **5.** M

Understanding the Story
1. The topic of his composition was My Greatest Accomplishment. **2.** His accomplishments were leaving Laos, swimming across the Mekhong River, coming to America, getting a job, going to school, and meeting new people. **3.** He thinks his greatest accomplishment is learning English. **4.** He told her that the composition was difficult to write. **5.** He said that because it's hard to measure everything you have done in your life.

Grammar
A. 1. Writing a composition isn't easy. **2.** Leaving Laos was hard. **3.** Swimming across the Mekhong River made me tired. **4.** Going to school makes me happy. **5.** Meeting new people every day is a great experience.

B. 1. I have done many things in my life. **2.** I have come a long way from home. **3.** I have gotten a job. **4.** I have seen many things. **5.** I have gone many places.